The Grapple with Emotions:

Using Brazilian Jiu-Jitsu
for Emotional Regulation in Kids

Joao Crus

Contents

Introduction

Imagine a world where children learn to channel their emotions through the discipline of martial arts. Where focus, resilience, and compassion become as instinctive as breathing. Imagine children who learn to fall and rise again, not with tears but with determination. Imagine young hearts discovering their personal strength to face challenges head-on rather than succumbing to fleeing temptations. This is not a mere dream but a reality I have witnessed time and again on the mats of my school in Austin, Texas.

How exactly can the gentle art of Brazilian Jiu-Jitsu (BJJ) unlock the boundless potential of our children's emotions? It's my pleasure to share the answers from my in-depth personal experience in the pages of this book. Over two decades of dedication as a practitioner, coach, and trainer of coaches has forged me into a passionate steward of this profound martial art. I know from my own personal transformation and witnessing that of countless students over the years that BJJ has the power to transform the fabric of our emotions through its physical practice.

My personal journey to discover and embrace Brazilian Jiu-Jitsu began in the heart of the bustling streets of Rio de Janeiro, where the rhythm of life pulses with a fierce intensity, and where I moved alone at the age of 17 from Brasilia, where I was born. My life as a competitive athlete began in the water. I competed as a swimmer in my youth, windsurfing and sailing as a young adult, winning the amateur circuit three times in Caribbean competitions. My first foray into martial arts was not actually BJJ but learning the precise karate techniques. During my 6 years competing in karate, I won five state tournaments and placed second in two national tournaments.

Before testing my black belt in Karate, I stumbled upon Brazilian Jiu-Jitsu and began secretly attending classes while still training in Karate. I started training secretly because my Karate instructor, at the time, was jealous of my interest in Jiu-Jitsu. Once I had a taste of BJJ, I lost my desire to progress past the rank of brown belt and began training BJJ full-time in 1998. I secured a blue belt under the tutelage of Leonardo Castello Branco, a legendary BJJ black belt and Pro MMA fighter in Rio. This marked the beginning of a lifelong commitment to mastery and teaching. I also had the enormous honor of becoming a direct disciple and friend of the legendary Carlson Gracie and becoming a BJJ instructor under him.

It is through both Gracie and Branco's inspiring influence and my silent embrace of the BJJ mat that I have found my true calling. I have been a passionate advocate of what's possible to achieve physically and emotionally through BJJ ever since.

Transitioning to life in the United States brought new horizons for me. Here, I founded my BJJ schools in Austin and Dripping

Springs. While my schools offer classes for adults and children, the most compelling chapter of my story occurred when I focused on children and nurturing the next generation of practitioners. Witnessing their struggles, their triumphs, and the remarkable emotional transformation fostered through BJJ has been my greatest achievement. Every day, I witness young souls' metamorphosis from chaos to control and uncertainty to confidence. It's what led me to the profound realization that Brazilian Jiu-Jitsu is so much more than a sport; it's a tool for shaping the heart and mind with unparalleled lessons in emotional regulation, discipline, and resilience.

As I honed my expertise as a coach and continued to refine my instructional techniques for children, I was frequently sought after by top BJJ coaches and school owners nationally and overseas, seeking advice on starting their own programs for children. Through creating instructional DVDs and conducting seminars across Europe, I have endeavored to spread the gospel of BJJ far and wide.

My book is an invitation to parents, educators, and coaches to join me on a transformative journey that promises not just skills for the mat but for life. As you explore the chapters within, I invite you to read with your mind and heart open. As you will discover, the lessons of Brazilian Jiu-Jitsu extend beyond the technical to touch upon the essence of what it means to be human. We will explore the intricate connection between physical movement and emotional well-being, the discipline of training and its impact on focus and decision-making, and the role of community in fostering resilience and overcoming adversity.

The insights and strategies shared here are not just for your child but for you as well. Embrace them, and together, let us unlock the boundless potential that lies within the gentle art of Brazilian Jiu-Jitsu.

BJJ History & Core Principles

The Origin of Brazilian Jiu-Jitsu

In the early 20th century, the vibrant streets of Rio de Janeiro became the crucible setting for a martial art that would eventually traverse the globe, embedding itself in the hearts of millions. This was Brazilian Jiu-Jitsu, a combat sport that evolved through a series of adaptations, challenges, and triumphs, much like the human condition. The word "jiu-jitsu" derives from the Japanese "Jū," meaning "gentle," and "Jutsu," meaning "art;" essentially, jiu-jitsu translates as "gentle art" and is understood as using your opponent's strength to your advantage.

Brazilian Jiu-Jitsu is a tale of physical prowess crossing paths with the indomitable spirit of resilience, making it a perfect metaphor for our emotional journeys, especially in childhood. As we delve into the history of BJJ, we uncover the roots of discipline and emotional regulation inherent in the practice, offering invaluable lessons for the present and future.

These lessons are the cornerstone of our exploration in this book. Why does history matter now? Understanding where we come from is pivotal to navigating where we are headed. In a world where children grapple with unprecedented challenges and pressures, the teachings of BJJ offer a light of hope. The discipline instilled by regular practice, the camaraderie fostered among peers, and the self-esteem built through incremental achievements are more than just benefits; they are necessities for emotional regulation and well-being. As we move from the historical to the contemporary, it becomes evident that the principles underlying BJJ are not confined to the past. They live and thrive in the communities and schools that practice this martial art today.

The evolution of BJJ is intrinsically linked to the Japanese martial art of Judo, which found its way to Brazil in the early 1900s, thanks to Mitsuyo Maeda, a Judo master. Maeda's teachings were embraced by Carlos Gracie, a Brazilian scholar and entrepreneur, who saw in them a method of self-defense and a way of life. This marked the birth of Brazilian Jiu-Jitsu, as Carlos and his brother Helio Gracie adapted and refined these techniques, laying down the foundations for what would become a global phenomenon. The Gracie brothers' refinement and adaptation of Judo was rooted in modifications to shift the focus from speed and strength to timing and leverage. These were motivated by Helio Gracie's own personal physical frailty from illness as a way for physically weak people to be able to apply Judo techniques successfully.

Carlos Gracie and his brothers opened the first Jiu-Jitsu academy in Brazil, nurturing a space where physical combat turned into a dance of control, leverage, strategy, efficiency, and resilience. The mats became arenas where victories were measured not by the ability to overpower an opponent but by the capacity to control one's emotions, to remain calm under pressure, to be strategic using leverage and efficiency, and to exhibit resilience in the face of defeat.

The Core Principles of Jiu-Jitsu

Embarking on this journey requires understanding the core principles that distinguish the martial art of BJJ: control, leverage, and efficiency over brute strength. These principles are pivotal to mastering BJJ's physical aspects and serve as metaphors for managing emotions. In essence, the practice of BJJ mirrors the emotional regulation process, making it an ideal framework for teaching children how to navigate their feelings. To appreciate the depth of this metaphor, let's break down the principles that form the bedrock of BJJ. Each of these words carries a weight of meaning on the mats and in the emotional arena of a child's life.

Control. BJJ is about mastering yourself before attempting to master an opponent. It's the ability to dictate the pace and direction of the match, relying on skill and strategy rather than force. This concept translates seamlessly into emotional regulation, where control is about recognizing your feelings without letting them dictate your actions impulsively.

Leverage. When practicing BJJ, you learn how to strategically use force strategically, ensuring minimal effort yields maximum effect and achieves a desired outcome with the least wasted energy. It's about using the opponent's strength and momentum against them. In emotional terms, leverage is about finding and utilizing one's strengths in challenging situations, turning potential setbacks into opportunities for growth, and using one's understanding of personal strengths and weaknesses to navigate difficult situations.

Efficiency. Practicing efficiency in BJJ involves choosing the most effective techniques for the situation at hand. Similarly, emotional efficiency is about dealing with feelings and conflicts in a way that resolves them without unnecessary stress or energy expenditure.

Consider the scenario where a child feels overwhelmed by anger. In BJJ, this emotion could equate to an opponent's aggressive advance. Just as a practitioner uses control to stay calm, leverage to turn the situation to their advantage, and efficiently respond effectively, a child can learn to manage their anger similarly. Instead of lashing out, they can recognize their feelings (control), use calming strategies (leverage), and express themselves in a constructive, assertive manner (efficiency), thereby learning to bounce back from emotional upheavals and gain resilience.

Resilience is a trait cultivated through the practice of BJJ's core principles. It's the ability to bounce back from setbacks, learn from defeat and persist in facing challenges. Emotionally, resilience equips children with the strength to face their problems, learn from their experiences, and continue moving forward. By linking these terms to familiar concepts, we bridge the gap between the mats and the emotional landscape of a child's life.

This metaphorical framework extends beyond individual emotions, offering a blueprint for daily navigating the complex web of social interactions and personal challenges children face. By understanding and applying the principles of BJJ, children can develop a toolkit for emotional regulation that is both practical and profound, building mental toughness, resilience, and a problem-solving mindset, which are crucial for emotional well-being.

The practice of Brazilian Jiu-Jitsu is a mirror reflecting the trials and triumphs of the human spirit, a microcosm of the emotional battles we face. As we delve deeper into BJJ techniques and stories, let us remember that the ultimate goal is not to foster future champions of the sport. Still, champions of life are equipped with the emotional intelligence and resilience to face and grapple with whatever challenges come their way.

Emotional Strength

Jiu-Jitsu and the Mind: Building a Resilient Psyche & Growth Mindset

In the tapestry of human experience, emotions play a central role, shaping our reactions, decision-making, and interactions with others. Like a complex dance, our emotions require understanding and finesse to navigate effectively. This is where the practice of BJJ emerges as a potent tool for managing emotions, building mental toughness, and developing a problem-solving mindset, which is crucial for emotional well-being.

BJJ is about the measured application of force and technique, a direct parallel to managing emotions, where control involves recognizing and modulating one's emotional responses. A child learning to maintain composure during a challenging BJJ role is cultivating the same skill required to stay calm during an emotional upheaval. In the context of BJJ, this refers to strategically using an opponent's strength against them.

Children learn to identify their emotional triggers and use strategies to counteract them, turning potential emotional breakdowns into opportunities for growth. They learn to focus on achieving goals with minimal wasted effort. BJJ means executing the most effective move at the right time. Emotionally, it addresses feelings or conflicts directly and constructively without unnecessary drama or escalation. While not a physical technique, this is a critical outcome of BJJ training. It's about bouncing back from defeats, learning from mistakes, and persevering.

Likewise, mastering a new move or technique offers tangible proof of their capabilities, bolstering their self-esteem and resilience. This psychological fortification is crucial, particularly in an era where children's mental health appears increasingly fragile. By providing a consistent and rewarding challenge, BJJ nurtures a 'growth mindset' – the belief that abilities can be developed through dedication and hard work.

Emotionally, this growth mindset and resilience equip children to face disappointments and setbacks with a positive attitude, learning from each experience. Through the lens of these criteria, the similarities between BJJ and emotional regulation become striking. Both require awareness, strategy, and adapting to changing circumstances. For instance, a child who learns to escape a difficult position on the mat simultaneously learns resilience to navigate challenging emotional situations.

While BJJ is a physical engagement with clear rules and boundaries, emotional regulation involves navigating the more nebulous realm of feelings and interpersonal dynamics. The concrete feedback of a successful BJJ maneuver does not always have a direct counterpart in the more subjective experiences of managing emotions. This difference underscores the importance of guided practice and reflection in learning emotional regulation as a coach provides feedback and instruction in BJJ.

Discipline: The Foundation of Growth

My journey of competing in a number of sports in Brazil gave me a very personal, profound understanding of the role of discipline in personal development. Competing in windsurfing, I learned the necessity of focus in training. Competing in Karate, where I practiced 2 hrs./day for 6 years, I learned discipline. After discovering my ultimate calling, Brazilian Jiu-Jitsu, where I earned my black belt, my discipline is now focused on how I teach and share my passion for the sport with children and adults and pay forward to attaining discipline in those I coach.

I remember two siblings I coached in Rio, Lucas and Sofia, who joined the gym with contrasting dispositions. Lucas, eight at the time, carried the weight of unchanneled energy and impulsive actions, while Sofia, who was ten, was the embodiment of withdrawn silence, her emotions locked behind a facade of apathy. The challenge was clear: I needed to leverage the structured discipline of BJJ to guide each of these young minds toward the distinct types of emotional regulation that they each needed through the structured discipline of BJJ.

I'm generally wired to be meticulous, and I also believe it's essential to incorporate compassion when teaching. My coaching approach combines these two things. For Lucas, I encouraged him to become a canvas for channeling his boundless energy into focused movements. Each roll, each grappling session, was a lesson in restraint, teaching him that true strength lies in controlled action. On the other hand, Sofia's journey was about unlocking the gates to her emotions. I set about, allowing and encouraging her to express herself through the fluid motions of BJJ. The mat became her safe space, where her vulnerability was not a weakness but a bridge to understanding her own strength.

Months turned into years, and the transformation was undeniable. Lucas learned the value of patience, and his once erratic energy became a focused force that he wielded with precision. With each roll and submission, Sofia found her voice, her silent world blossoming into one where she could express herself freely, her confidence growing with every class. The results spoke volumes. Not only did their skills on the mat improve, as well as but so did their emotional well-being.

Their parents noticed changes at home and school; the siblings were more composed, more articulate about their feelings, and, most importantly, happier.

"What started as a simple desire for my daughter to learn self-defense skills became so much more. After seeing the benefits that Joao's classes provided my daughter, I enrolled my sons when they were old enough. Learning jiu-jitsu has allowed all three of my kids to stay calm in the face of physical and emotional adversity. That's a skill most adults never learn. The classes also improved their self-confidence, attentiveness, and respect for others. Those improvements were clear and visible even before they became proficient in their self-defense skills. Enrolling them in Joao's class was one of the best decisions I've ever made." Justin Nielsen (Parent)

Reflecting on their journey, I saw a broader picture emerge. Discipline, often misconstrued as mere obedience, was, in fact, the cornerstone of emotional growth. Through the structured environment of BJJ training, Lucas and Sofia learned the discipline of controlling their bodies while learning to understand and regulate their emotions.

I believe the essence of discipline is not about restrictions. True discipline is about the freedom to grow within a supportive framework. I often say to kids, "It's not about belts or trophies. It's about the journey, growth, and the lives we touch along the way."

Confidence Through Competence

The journey of emotional regulation through Brazilian Jiu-Jitsu is a universal tale of transformation and empowerment, one that finds its roots in the ancient art of BJJ yet stretches to touch the lives of children worldwide.

The story now turns a new page, exploring how mastery of BJJ techniques fosters a profound sense of confidence in young practitioners, enabling them to face life's myriad challenges with a positive mindset. In a world where children are increasingly confronted with high expectations and relentless social media pressure, I believe the need for solid emotional grounding has never been more critical.

While offering numerous benefits, the digital age has also escalated the pace of life, sometimes leaving our youngest members feeling overwhelmed and inadequate. We are all witness to the growing crisis of muted confidence among children, manifesting itself in anxiety, withdrawal, and fear of failure. This issue, if left unaddressed, has far-reaching consequences. Children lacking confidence may shy away from new opportunities, struggle with academic and social challenges, and become more susceptible to mental health issues. Their vast and untapped potential risks being stifled by the shadows of self-doubt and fear.

Gaining competence in the practice of Brazilian Jiu-Jitsu offers a very compelling solution and pathway to building confidence. Learning and mastering BJJ techniques provides children with tangible proof of their abilities, reinforcing the belief that they can overcome obstacles and achieve their goals. Implementing this solution begins with enrolling children in a BJJ program that emphasizes personal growth and emotional intelligence. Instructors play a crucial role, guiding students through the challenges of mastering new techniques, encouraging perseverance, and celebrating each milestone. These learning environments become microcosms of the broader world, where children learn to navigate challenges, face their fears, and emerge victorious.

Evidence of the efficacy of BJJ in building confidence is seen in the stories of countless young practitioners. Take, for example, the tale of Mia, a once timid girl who found her stride through BJJ. When she first started taking classes at my gym in Dripping Springs, she couldn't look anyone in the eye and frequently froze in uncertainty. Each technique she mastered, from escapes to submissions, was a step toward self-assurance. The mats became her stage, where she learned to assert herself, make decisions under pressure, and trust in her abilities. Her transformation was a testament to the power of confidence through competence.

While BJJ stands out as a potent solution, alternative approaches also hold merit. Activities like team sports, public speaking clubs, or creative arts programs can similarly contribute to building children's confidence. However, BJJ's unique advantage lies in its individual nature and a strong sense of community, providing a balanced environment for personal development.

The message is clear: confidence can absolutely be cultivated. Through the disciplined practice of Brazilian Jiu-Jitsu, children learn more than just self-defense; they learn to believe in themselves. This belief, once ignited, fuels their journey through life, empowering them to face challenges head-on with a can-do attitude. The mats may be the starting point, but the lessons learned ripple outward, influencing every aspect of their lives.

So, we circle back to the central question: How do we equip our children to navigate the complexities of the modern world with confidence and resilience?

It is my passionate belief that the answer requires us not to shield children from adversity, and doing this actually harms children by disempowering them. I believe it is essential for their emotional well-being and confidence in life that we empower children to confront adversity head-on. Through the art of BJJ, children learn that with dedication and perseverance, no challenge is insurmountable.

Gaining confidence through competence, every child is the hero of their own story, capable of incredible growth and transformation. And as they tie their belts, step onto the mats, and face their opponents, they're not just learning to grapple with others – they're learning to grapple with life itself. In every technique mastered, every fear faced, and every challenge overcome, they find the strength to say, "I can do this." This is the essence of confidence. Brazilian Jiu-Jitsu is powerful.

Fostering Independence on the Mat

Fostering independence in children is akin to planting a seed and nurturing it into a robust tree, grounded yet reaching skyward with strength and resilience. Brazilian Jiu-Jitsu acts as the fertile soil in this analogy, providing a structured yet dynamic environment where young minds can flourish, making decisions under pressure and cultivating a sense of self-reliance. This chapter delves into how BJJ paves the way for children to think and act independently, transforming challenges on the mat into emotional growth and maturity opportunities.

The goal is clear: to empower children with the tools they need to navigate the complexities of their emotions and social interactions, fostering a sense of independence that will serve them throughout their lives. This journey involves more than just learning to execute a perfect armbar or sweep; it's about developing the confidence to make decisions, the resilience to face setbacks, and the courage to trust one's abilities.

Before we step onto the mat, let's gather what we need. The prerequisites include an open mind, a willingness to embrace challenges, and a supportive environment that encourages exploration and learning. Parents, coaches, and the children play pivotal roles in this process, each contributing to the fertile ground for independence to grow. Imagine a path winding through a dense, uncharted forest. Initially, the way might seem daunting, obscured by shadows and uncertainty. Yet, with each step, the path becomes clearer, obstacles become stepping stones, and the forest reveals a landscape of possibilities.

The roadmap begins with creating a supportive environment, then moves through teaching decision-making skills, and, finally, celebrating autonomy. Creating a supportive environment is paramount. I'll touch on the importance of the coach and parent partnership later, but coaches and parents really must work together to ensure that the BJJ gym is a place where mistakes are viewed as learning opportunities, questions are encouraged, and every child feels valued and understood. This foundation sets the stage for independence to take root.

Teaching decision-making skills starts early in BJJ training. Children are encouraged to think on their feet — literally. During a roll, there's no time to look to a coach for answers; decisions must be made now. This process begins with simple choices, such as which technique to use in a given situation. It gradually becomes more complex as children learn to anticipate their partners' moves and plan their strategies accordingly. Fostering resilience is a natural extension of learning decision-making. Not every decision will lead to success on the mat, and that's okay. BJJ teaches children to view setbacks as temporary and approach problems with a mindset of perseverance and improvement. The resilience developed through these experiences is a critical component of emotional independence.

Celebrating autonomy takes place both on and off the mat. As children begin to trust in their abilities and confidently make decisions, it's important to recognize and celebrate these milestones. Whether successfully executing a new technique during sparring or choosing to face a challenging situation in their personal life with courage, these moments underscore the progress they've made toward becoming independent thinkers and doers. Embrace the journey. Be patient with it. Developing independence is a gradual process, filled with ups and downs. Encourage children to reflect on their experiences, learn from their mistakes, and savor their achievements.

Beware of the common urge to step in and solve problems for them. While it's natural to want to protect and help, learning to be independent involves grappling with challenges firsthand. Offer guidance but allow them the space to explore and find their own solutions. How do we know if we're making progress? Look for signs of increased confidence, a willingness to tackle new challenges, and a growing sense of responsibility for their actions and decisions. More than any medal or trophy, these indicators signify that a child is developing emotional independence that will support them throughout their lives. They simply cannot achieve this if the adults in their lives are hovering and solving things for them.

It's not uncommon for children to experience frustration or doubt on their journey toward independence. When this happens, we must remind them of their past successes and the progress they've made. Encourage them to view challenges as opportunities to learn and grow. If necessary, seek additional support from coaches or peers who can provide encouragement and perspective. Through their continued disciplined practice of Brazilian Jiu-Jitsu, children learn to face life's challenges head-on, equipped with the resilience, decision-making skills, and self-reliance they need to succeed. This is the essence of fostering independence on the mat.

Problem-Solving in Real-Time

As shared above, Brazilian Jiu-Jitsu fosters independence, providing children with a unique battleground to learn how to think on their feet. Let's dive further into the topic of BJJ and real-time problem solving and how it works as a sophisticated tool for sharpening and nurturing mental skills, especially in the young minds of children who extend far beyond the mats.

I've witnessed firsthand through my decades of coaching children in BJJ. Engaging in this martial art can significantly enhance a child's ability to analyze situations, anticipate outcomes, and devise strategies on the fly. This happens through the very nature of the sport—a dynamic interplay of moves and countermoves that demand quick thinking and rapid adaptation.

Children learn how to react to their opponent's movements, but more importantly – how to predict them, a skill paramount to developing advanced cognitive abilities. They are constantly faced with complex problems requiring immediate solutions— whether to escape a hold, counter an attack, or find the most effective way to achieve a submission. BJJ's inherent requirement for split-second decision-making under pressure simulates the high-stakes environments that children might face in real life. This experiential learning strengthens neural pathways associated with problem-solving, strategic planning, and spatial awareness. Moreover, the iterative process of trial and error, so central to BJJ, fosters an agile mindset adaptable to changing circumstances—a skill invaluable in all walks of life.

Skeptics might argue that BJJ's competitive nature could instill aggression or lead to undue stress in children, potentially overshadowing the cognitive benefits. Explorations indicate that BJJ when taught with an emphasis on respect, discipline, and control, can actually reduce aggression in children by providing a healthy outlet for their energy and teaching them the value of patience and persistence. Moreover, social interactions and camaraderie developed within BJJ classes promote empathy and understanding, complementing the development of conflict resolution skills. Additional supporting evidence comes from testimonials from parents and educators who have witnessed remarkable transformations in children engaged in BJJ.

Beyond the anecdotal, structured assessments have shown improvements in concentration, self-esteem, and academic performance among young BJJ practitioners. These benefits highlight the sport's role in fostering physical fitness and shaping well-rounded, mentally agile individuals. In conclusion, the assertion that BJJ training enhances cognitive skills in children, teaching them to analyze, anticipate, and strategize in real time, stands on solid ground.

The journey through BJJ is one of constant learning and adaptation, reflecting the unpredictability of life itself. Through the challenges faced on the mats, children develop a toolkit of cognitive skills that prepare them for the complexities of the world beyond. This is the essence of problem-solving in real-time, a testament to the profound impact of Brazilian Jiu-Jitsu on its youngest practitioners' developing minds. The empirical and anecdotal evidence reinforces the claim, painting a vivid picture of a martial art about much more than physical prowess—it is a forge for the mind, where the flames of challenge temper the steel of cognition and strategy.

Emotional Regulation

The Science of Sweat: Exercise and Emotion

The unique physical rigor and discipline of Brazilian Jiu-Jitsu can be particularly impactful for acting as a conduit for enhancing emotional stability. When children engage in the demanding workouts of BJJ, their bodies release a cocktail of hormones, including endorphins, dopamine, and serotonin. Known colloquially as the 'feel-good hormones,' these biochemical agents are potent mood lifters.

Studies have shown that regular physical activity can alleviate symptoms of depression and anxiety. In fact, a recent study published in Medical News Today showed that physical activity is 1.5 times more effective at reducing mild-to-moderate symptoms of depression, psychological stress, and anxiety than medication or cognitive behavior therapy.

This biochemical shift lays the groundwork for emotional stability, providing a natural buffer against the tumultuous seas of childhood and emotions. Delving deeper, BJJ's psychological benefits extend beyond a workout's immediate euphoria. The discipline instills a sense of achievement and self-efficacy in children.

Critics might argue that the competitive nature of BJJ could exacerbate stress and anxiety in some children, potentially undoing the emotional benefits. This viewpoint, while valid, overlooks the comprehensive approach that BJJ schools often take, emphasizing cooperation, respect, and mutual support among practitioners. Furthermore, a well-structured BJJ program can tailor the experience to individual needs, ensuring the focus remains on personal growth rather than competition.

Addressing these concerns, additional evidence supports BJJ's unique role in fostering social connections and a sense of community. Unlike traditional team sports, BJJ's dual focus on individual progress and group dynamics offers a unique social environment. Children learn to trust and rely on their peers, developing empathy and social skills in a context that celebrates diversity and mutual respect. The culmination of biochemical, psychological, and social factors paints a compelling picture of BJJ's role in emotional regulation. Challenging the body fortifies the mind, creating a resilient and adaptive emotional landscape in children to prepare them better to face life's challenges with confidence and grace.

Building Emotional Stamina with Endurance & Breath Control

The parallels between enduring a strenuous BJJ session and navigating emotional turmoil are striking. Both scenarios demand a presence of mind, a willingness to face discomfort head-on, patience to work through it, and a deep understanding of oneself. As practitioners grapple with their opponents in BJJ, they learn the importance of breathing, maintaining focus, and staying calm under pressure. These lessons translate seamlessly into emotional scenarios, where breathing deeply, focusing on solutions, and remaining calm can turn the tides of an emotional storm.

During the matches, the coaches instruct the children to breathe deep and slowly to remain calm and present on the tasks they are involved in, like focusing on escaping from a hold on the ground or taking advantage of good positioning to apply a submission.

Contrastingly, the physical and emotional domains diverge in the immediacy of feedback and visibility of progress. Physical endurance is often measurable through tangible performance, stamina, and strength improvements. Emotional stamina, however, unfolds internally, making its growth harder to quantify. This distinction underscores the nuanced nature of emotional resilience, a journey marked by personal milestones rather than universal benchmarks.

As we forge ahead, let us carry the lessons of the mats into our daily lives and embrace the grind of gaining physical endurance and nurturing emotional resilience along the way. In the heart of every challenge lies an opportunity to grow stronger inside and out. In the dance between physical exertion and emotional resilience, we find a harmony that propels us forward, ready to face the world with a steadfast heart and an unyielding spirit.

Specifically, during training, BJJ's emphasis on mindfulness, focus, and present-moment awareness enhances practitioners' emotional regulation skills. The mats become a microcosm of life's broader emotional landscape, where each roll teaches practitioners to navigate their emotions with the same dexterity they apply to escape a tight hold.

The Joy of Movement: BJJ as Play

This is a common scene in my studio. Children, clad in their Gi, lined up with eyes gleaming with excitement and perhaps a touch of nervousness. Many of them have more energy than they know what to do with it. Many parents enroll their children in Brazilian Jiu-Jitsu to channel their child's boundless energy at home and school into something constructive.

Play, in its purest form, is an expression of joy, a venture into the realms of imagination and exploration. Brazilian Jiu-Jitsu offers just that but with a twist. It teaches its practitioners, especially the young ones, that within the framework of play lies the potential for joy alongside profound learning and growth.

My first lesson with students was not through a lecture but, most often, through a game of 'tag' with a Jiu-Jitsu spin. The goal is simple: touch your partner's knee without letting them touch yours. It inevitably becomes an exhilarating chase for the kids with an underlying lesson in strategy, balance, and control.

In their pursuit of victory, they discover the joy of movement, the thrill of anticipation, and the satisfaction of a challenge met.

The lessons from games and exercises on the mats don't end there. The kids learn to respect their instructors and each other, understanding that every partner is a teacher in disguise. They learn about perseverance when they experience joy after mastering a technique seemingly out of reach after days, sometimes weeks, of practice. The mats become a canvas for these young minds, a place where failure isn't feared; it's embraced as a step toward growth.

One student in particular, Peter, noticeably benefited from experiencing BJJ exercises as games. He initially viewed setbacks with frustration and then, after some time, began to see them as puzzles to be solved, challenges to be met with curiosity and determination. This transformation into forming a more flexible, resilient growth mindset was not lost on his parents, who noticed a newfound calmness in him, a reflective quality that was previously foreign to his restless nature. They saw him approach homework, chores, and even disagreements with a level of patience and strategy that mirrored his approach on the mat.

What does this tell us about the universal truths embedded in the art of Brazilian Jiu-Jitsu? It underscores the notion that play, guided by purpose and understanding, can be a powerful catalyst for emotional and psychological growth.

With its blend of physicality, strategy, and camaraderie, Brazilian Jiu-Jitsu offers a unique avenue for children to navigate the complexities of emotions and interactions with a grounded sense of self and a joyful heart. The joy of movement in BJJ is more than just playing. It is a gateway to understanding oneself and the world with a balanced mind and an open heart. It teaches that true strength lies not in dominance but in graceful give and take, in laughter shared after a roll, and in the quiet confidence that comes from knowing you are part of something larger than yourself.

Peter's story is one of many, a testament to the beauty and depth of Brazilian Jiu-Jitsu as a form of play. It invites us to look beyond the surface and see the mats as a place for physical training and a playground for life's most valuable lessons.

Emotional Intelligence

Empathy, Patience & Listening through Sparring

A transformation occurs in the heart of a bustling dojo, where the sounds of effort and the soft thud of bodies meeting mats fill the air. It's not just about the physical prowess children gain here; it's about the emotional intelligence they develop, threaded through each lesson like a silent, guiding force. This is the essence of Brazilian Jiu-Jitsu - a journey not just for the body but for the mind and heart. At the core of this transformative journey is the proposition that BJJ training serves as an unparalleled medium for developing emotional intelligence in children, teaching them to read situations and react appropriately, akin to reading an opponent on the mat.

This claim is rooted not in mere conjecture but in the concrete experiences of young practitioners and the observations of those who guide them. The primary evidence supporting this claim emerges from the structured environment of BJJ training itself, specifically from the way I planned the curriculum. Within the structured environment of BJJ training, children learn patience, empathy, and the value of listening to their coaches and peers. They engage in a constant dialogue of action and reaction, learning to anticipate and adapt, mirroring emotional interaction complexities in their daily lives.

31

Consider the ritual of sparring, known in BJJ as "rolling." This practice is about understanding your own limits and recognizing others' strengths and weaknesses. Empathy is nurtured in the clasp of hands, and the meeting of eyes, and children learn to understand and respect their peers' strengths and struggles. This intricate and nuanced process unfolds on the mats, weaving a tapestry of emotional intelligence alongside physical prowess. Children who learn to navigate a role simultaneously learn to navigate their emotions. They learn that aggression might not always be the answer, that sometimes yielding can lead to a better position, and that resilience often leads to improvement.

The art is often described as a physical chess game, where foresight, adaptability, and understanding of one's opponent are key. Far from encouraging aggression, BJJ teaches children the importance of calmness and clarity under pressure.

When two children bow and engage, they embark on a journey of mutual discovery. One might notice how their partner's breathing changes with anxiety or exertion or how a slight hesitation might hint at uncertainty. These observations, though subtle, are the first steps toward empathy. They learn to read emotions as well as movements, understanding that behind every action on the mat, there's a corresponding internal process. Diving deeper, it becomes evident how this understanding translates into respect and empathy.

For instance, when a child realizes their partner is struggling with a particular move or grappling with self-doubt, their response often shifts from competition to support. This transformation is palpable. They may offer a word of encouragement, adjust their intensity, or share a technique post-match. Through these actions, children not only show empathy but reinforce it within themselves, learning that another way of exhibiting martial arts strength is to uplift and understand others.

As they bow to their partners at the end of a sparring session, these young practitioners acknowledge the physical contest between one another and a shared journey of growth and mutual respect, showing a greater capacity for empathy. We like to encourage post-sparring discussions, where children share what they have learned from their partners and themselves to reinforce emotional intelligence. Coaches encourage reflection on choices made for techniques and, through the process of open discussion, foster understanding and connection with their peers on a deeper level.

It's in these moments that children articulate their empathy, acknowledging their partners' challenges and celebrating their strengths. One space at a time, they learn to see beyond themselves, understanding and respecting their peers with compassion in a way that transcends the mats.

I love hearing stories from parents and instructors who witness remarkable transformations in children who practice BJJ. They speak of shy children who learn to express themselves more confidently, of bullies who learn the value of kindness, and of every child in between who learns that true empathy lies in understanding someone else's struggle as if it were their own.

The Respectful Warrior: Cultivating Honor and Integrity

You bow as you step onto the mat, a sacred space where respect reigns supreme. From the moment you don that crisp white go, you enter a world governed by an unspoken code – a code that demands humility, discipline, and an unwavering commitment to growth, both on and off the mat. As you bow to your instructor and training partners, you acknowledge their presence and pay homage to a lineage that stretches back centuries, a legacy forged by warriors who understood that true strength lies in the mastery of oneself. In the gentle art of Jiu-Jitsu, you quickly learn that ego has no place.

The mats are a great equalizer, where rank and status hold little sway. Instead, the purity of your technique, the depth of your understanding, and the strength of your character determine your progress. With each roll, each exchange of technique, you engage in a sacred dance of respect – a silent acknowledgment that your training partner is not an opponent to be conquered but a fellow traveler on the path of self-discovery. Every tap is a humble admission of momentary victory, a gesture of gratitude for the lessons imparted, and a reminder that true mastery lies in the pursuit of constant improvement, not the fleeting gratification of victory.

In this crucible of respect, children learn invaluable lessons in controlling emotions, channeling frustration into focus, and embracing the lessons that every setback has to offer. As they bow to their instructors and training partners, they imbibe the sacred rituals of respect – rituals that instill a deep reverence for the traditions that have shaped this art and a humility that serves as a bulwark against the insidious whispers of ego and entitlement. With every tap, every submission gracefully accepted, they learn that failure is a stepping stone on the growth path. They learn that true warriors are not defined by the number of victories they accrue but by the resilience with which they face adversity and the grace with which they acknowledge the achievements of others. In this sanctuary of respect, the seeds of character are sown – seeds that blossom into traits of integrity, discipline, and an unwavering commitment to personal growth.

As children navigate the treacherous waters of adolescence and beyond, these lessons become beacons, guiding them through the turbulent currents of peer pressure, temptation, and the siren call of instant gratification. In a world that often celebrates the loudest and the brashest, the mats offer a sanctuary where quiet strength reigns supreme. The depth of one's convictions is infinitely more powerful, especially– convictions rooted in a bedrock of respect for themselves, for others, and for the sacred traditions that have shaped their journey. As they progress through the ranks of BJJ, each new belt serves as a symbol of the character they have forged – a testament to the countless battles waged within, the moments of self-doubt conquered, and the lessons of humility and respect that have become woven into the very fabric of their being.

With every bow, every tap, every silent acknowledgment of the journey ahead, children are imbued with a profound understanding that the ritual of respect is not merely a ritual but a way of life – a path that leads to greatness, both on the mats and in the ever-shifting landscapes of their lives. As they step off the mats, these young warriors carry with them a quiet confidence, a sense of purpose that transcends the boundaries of sport. They have glimpsed the power of respect and wield it as a talisman against the temptations of ego, entitlement, and the digital life paradigm we live in now that fosters a perceived need for the siren call of instant gratification.

In a world that often celebrates the loudest and the brashest, these children stand as living embodiments of a profound truth: that true strength lies not in the force of one's grip but in the depth of one's character, the resilience of one's spirit, and the unwavering commitment to walking the path of honor, integrity, and respect. In the gentle art of Jiu-Jitsu, they have discovered a world where respect reigns supreme – a world that shapes not only their physical prowess but also the very essence of who they are destined to become.

Routine and Ritual: The Significance of the Gi, Bowing, and Lineups

In the world of Brazilian Jiu-Jitsu (BJJ), the Gi stands as a symbol that transcends mere attire. To the uninitiated, this traditional uniform might seem no different from any other piece of sportswear. However, the Gi represents a profound journey of growth, discipline, and community for those who train and find solace on the mats.

At its core, the Gi is a sturdy garment designed for the rigors of grappling. Comprising a heavy cotton jacket, reinforced trousers, and a belt that signifies rank, this attire is engineered to withstand BJJ's pulling, gripping, and intense physical engagement. The belt, tied around the waist with a specific knot, not only keeps the jacket closed but also serves as a marker of the practitioner's progress and skill level. Digging deeper, each element of the Gi carries weight. The fabric's durability mirrors the resilience BJJ instills in its practitioners. Beyond indicating rank, the belt wraps around the wearer with the weight of their journey. Each stripe and color change is a testament to hours of dedication, learning, and overcoming challenges.

Historically, the Gi traces its roots back to traditional Japanese kimono. It was adapted for the martial art of Judo in the late 19th century and subsequently adopted by Brazilian Jiu-Jitsu. This evolution speaks to the Gi's role in bridging cultures and histories, embodying a legacy of martial arts that spans continents and centuries. Placing the Gi within the broader framework of BJJ, it becomes clear that this uniform acts as a rite of passage. Donning the Gi is a ritual that prepares the mind and body for the lessons ahead, fostering a sense of pride and belonging among practitioners.

Stepping onto the mat in a Gi, one joins a global community bound by shared values and experiences. In children, the impact of wearing a Gi can be transformative. Through the lens of emotional regulation, the Gi serves as a tangible reminder of the discipline, respect, and focus BJJ cultivates. It's not uncommon to witness a shy child's posture straighten as they tie their belt, a physical manifestation of the confidence and sense of achievement BJJ nurtures.

The real-world applications of training in a Gi extend beyond physical skills. Children learn to navigate their emotions, channeling frustration or anger into determination and resilience. The act of caring for their Gi, keeping it clean and mended, teaches responsibility and respect for their belongings and, by extension, their environment and peers.

Misconceptions about the Gi abound. Some view it as an unnecessary barrier to entry, a costly and complicated piece of equipment. Yet, the Gi's role in promoting equality and unity cannot be overstated. On the mat, differences in background, status, or strength blur; everyone wears the same uniform, learns the same techniques, and faces the same challenges. Why does this matter? BJJ and its traditions offer a counter-narrative in a world where children are bombarded with messages about quick success and superficial achievements. As an integral part of this narrative, the Gi reinforces the values of hard work, persistence, and mutual respect.

Consider the moment a child receives their first Gi. The excitement in their eyes is palpable as they slip their arms into the sleeves, a mix of anticipation and pride. This moment, simple yet profound, marks the beginning of a journey in BJJ and life.

"A black belt is a white belt who never gives up" is a common saying in the BJJ community, underscoring the essence of the journey. In its simplicity and complexity, the Gi is a constant companion on this path, growing and evolving with the practitioner. In conclusion, the significance of the Gi in Brazilian Jiu-Jitsu, especially for children, cannot be overstated. It is a symbol of the journey, a teacher of valuable life lessons, and a bridge connecting the past with the present. Through the discipline of caring for and training in the Gi, children learn the power of routine and ritual while developing physical and emotional resilience and gaining a sense of communal belonging and achievement. In the tapestry of BJJ, the Gi is not just a piece of fabric but a thread that weaves together the physical, emotional, and communal aspects of martial arts, creating a vibrant and enduring picture.

Bowing and Lineups

In the dojo, where the air is thick with anticipation and the mats witness countless tales of perseverance, rituals of respect stand as the cornerstone of Brazilian Jiu-Jitsu. Among these, the formal practice and ritual of bowing to the mat and lining up according to rank are formalities that serve as profound practices that instill discipline, honor, and a deep sense of respect. These rituals, woven into the very fabric of BJJ training, serve as a constant reminder of the rich heritage of martial arts and the values it seeks to impart.

At the heart of these practices lies the concept of respect—a multifaceted gem that shines through the actions and attitudes of practitioners. Bowing to the mat, a gesture that might seem simple at first glance is imbued with significance. It is an acknowledgment of the sacred space where individuals come together to learn, struggle, grow, and, ultimately, transform.

This bow is a physical act that symbolizes humility. It serves as a momentary pause where one leaves the outside world behind and enters a realm dedicated to the pursuit of mastery and self-improvement.

Lining up according to rank further reinforces this culture of respect, creating a visual representation of the journey each practitioner undertakes. This orderly formation speaks volumes from the eager white belts, fresh on their path, to the seasoned black belts, who have weathered countless storms. It is a testament to the hard work, dedication, and perseverance required to ascend through the ranks. The message is clear for the young practitioners observing and participating in this ritual: respect is earned, and growth is a continuous journey.

Imagine a young child, Gi tied neatly, standing in line, eyes wide with a mix of reverence and anticipation. They watch as their peers and instructors bow to the mat, a silent yet powerful gesture that resonates deeply. In this moment, the child learns a valuable lesson —not with words, but through the silent observation of the group's collective action. They understand that respect is not just given; it is demonstrated through one's actions and attitudes, both on and off the mat.

One discovers a rich tapestry of perspectives and interpretations by diving deeper into these practices. Some view the bow as a direct link to BJJ's roots in Japanese martial arts, a nod to the tradition and history that shape the discipline.

Others see it as a personal commitment to uphold the values of BJJ—integrity, humility, and respect. Similarly, the lineup is seen by many as a visual guide, a reminder that progress is possible with effort and time and that everyone's journey is unique yet interconnected.

Brazilian Jiu-Jitsu plays a pivotal role in developing discipline and respect among children. Anecdotal evidence abounds, with countless stories of transformation—shy children finding their voice, unruly kids learning self-control, and young minds developing a newfound appreciation for respect and discipline.

Complex terms like "hierarchy" and "tradition" are often thrown around in discussions about these rituals. At their core, these concepts are simple. Hierarchy in BJJ is not about superiority but about recognizing and honoring each individual's journey and contributions. Tradition is the thread that connects the present to the past, a way of preserving and honoring the legacy of those who paved the way. I view the rituals of respect in BJJ—bowing to the mat and lining up according to rank—as far more than mere formalities. They are integral to the fabric of BJJ, serving as daily reminders of the values the martial art seeks to instill. For children, these ritual routine practices are powerful as routines and lessons in respect, discipline, and the continuous journey of growth. As they bow to the mat and stand in line, they learn to honor the past, engage with the present, and look forward to the future with humility and determination.

Friendship & Community: Bonds Built on the Mat

In the heart of Rio de Janeiro, under the sweltering heat of the summer sun, I have memories of a group of children gathering on the worn mats of a modest dojo. Though faded and patched in places, their Gi's were worn with pride. Among them was a boy, Pedro, whose eyes gleamed with an unspoken determination. Though slightly awkward, his stance hints at a budding confidence that transcends his years.

Today, Pedro's journey on the mat intertwines with that of Sofia, a girl whose fierce spirit is matched only by her nimble agility. As their instructor, I watched from the sidelines, my heart swelling with pride. These children, each from vastly different walks of life, found common ground in BJJ. Here, on these mats, social barriers dissolve, friendships are forged, and a unique family is born.

Each fall, each submission, teaches them about getting back up, about perseverance, and about the strength that lies within. It's a lesson I learned years ago that transformed my life. Once a shy boy who would flinch at the slightest touch, Pedro now engages his opponents with a focus that belies his age. Sofia, who struggled to find her place in a world that often seemed too large and intimidating, moves with confidence that commands respect. Their transformation is a testament to BJJ's power as a personal growth tool.

As the children pair up, laughter and cheers fill the air, painting a vivid picture of camaraderie. Here, in this dojo, there are students, brothers and sisters, mentors, and proteges. The bonds formed on these mats are unbreakable, forged in sweat and perseverance. In the beginning, Pedro and Sofia's interactions were marked by tentative smiles and awkward silences. Now, they share strategies, celebrate each other's victories, and console one another in defeat. Their friendship, born from mutual respect and shared struggles, exemplifies the profound connections BJJ nurtures.

And what about the mentors, the seasoned practitioners who guide these young warriors? Their role is pivotal. They are role models who embody the values of respect, humility, and discipline. Their guidance extends beyond the mats, touching lives in profound and unexpected ways. Take, for instance, the story of Carlos, a former competitor turned instructor. His journey, marked by triumphs and setbacks, resonates deeply with children. Through his stories, they learn that the path to success is not linear but a tapestry of experiences that shape us. Carlos, a Jiu-Jitsu instructor, has a captivating history that inspires his students. Born with a natural talent for martial arts, Carlos began his journey as a competitor at a young age. With dedication and hard work, he achieved remarkable success in various tournaments, earning a reputation as a formidable fighter and champion.

However, Carlos' path to success was not without challenges. Along the way, he encountered setbacks and losses that tested his resilience. Once, in a tournament, he broke an arm in one final fight, which made him lose the tournament; on another occasion, he got hurt during the preparation for a tournament 3 days before the event and shouldn't have gone competing. He did anyway and was defeated earlier in his bracket. He never gave up, even with all the setbacks presented to him. These experiences taught him valuable lessons about perseverance and the importance of embracing failure as a stepping stone toward growth.

After a particularly difficult defeat, Carlos decided to shift his focus from competing to teaching. He realized his true passion lay in sharing his knowledge and helping others discover their potential. Carlos embarked on a new chapter in his life as a Jiu-Jitsu instructor with this newfound purpose.

As an instructor, Carlos dedicated himself to nurturing his students' skills and instilling discipline, respect, and perseverance in them. Through his own stories of triumphs and setbacks, he inspired his students to embrace the journey of self-improvement, understanding that success is not solely measured by victories but by personal growth achieved along the way.

Carlos' ability to connect with his students profoundly stems from his own experiences. He understands their struggles and uses his journey as a testament to the power of resilience and determination. His students look up to him not only as a skilled instructor but also as a mentor who guides them through the ups and downs of life.

Through Carlos' teachings, the children learn that true success is not defined by external accolades but by the strength of character developed through hard work, perseverance, and the ability to bounce back from setbacks. Carlos' story is a constant reminder that the path to success is not always linear but a tapestry of experiences that shape and mold us into the best versions of ourselves.

Carlos's mentorship is a beacon of hope, a reminder that every struggle is an opportunity for growth. The dojo, thus, becomes a microcosm of life, a place where lessons learned on the mat ripple outwards, influencing families, schools, and communities. It's a testament to the transformative power of BJJ, a sport that teaches self-awareness, empathy, and the strength to face life's challenges. So, as we delve deeper into the world of BJJ and its impact on emotional regulation in children, let us not forget the stories of Pedro and Sofia. Their journey is a mirror reflecting the universal struggles and triumphs of childhood, a narrative that transcends the mats and touches the very core of our beings.

Their story only scratches the surface. As you turn the pages of this book, you'll discover more of the science behind the art, the psychology that underpins the techniques, and the heartwarming stories of transformation that abound in the world of BJJ. You'll learn how this ancient martial art is shaping the leaders of tomorrow, instilling in them values that will guide them through life's myriad challenges.

Welcome to the BJJ family. A family built not on blood but on bonds that are just as strong. Here, on the mats, we grapple not just with our opponents but with our emotions, learning to master them with the same finesse with which we execute a perfectly timed sweep or submission. This is the journey we embark on together. A journey that promises not just skill but wisdom. Not just victories but growth.

Leadership and Ro2le Models

My personal journey from Rio to Austin is a testament to the transformative power of BJJ. My experiences, complete with both victories and hard-earned lessons, form the bedrock of my teaching philosophy that emphasizes the holistic development of children. Leveraging my deep understanding of BJJ and personal study of child psychology, I have crafted a training program in which I incorporate stories from my own life, including tales of triumphs and setbacks, into my lessons.

Yes, all of our jobs as coaches require us to be role models for children. But the real magic happens on the mats when we encourage more senior students to lead by example. These young leaders, many of whom have walked the path from timidity to confidence, become role models for the newcomers. The interactions, though seemingly simple - a helping hand here, a word of encouragement there - are profound. They are the threads that weave the fabric of our dojo, where every child feels seen, heard, and valued, and victory comes from uplifting others as we celebrate each other's achievements.

The posters and decorations in my studio that capture victories and moments of camaraderie serve as symbols of a journey shared and challenges overcome together. While deeply personal, this journey connects to a larger narrative - the role of martial arts in shaping better individuals and, by extension, a better society. It's a narrative that I live by through my life work and what I hope to contribute to everyday through my dedication to my students.

Conflict Resolution on and off the mat

In a society increasingly quick to polarize and escalate disputes, the ability to peacefully resolve differences is a skill that seems to be fading into the background. The consequences of neglecting this crucial aspect of human interaction are dire. Without the tools to mediate and resolve disputes, children risk becoming adults who struggle with communication, harbor resentment, and potentially escalate conflicts to destructive ends. If left unchecked, this cycle of misunderstanding and aggression has the power to fracture communities and deepen societal divides.

Getting inside the dojo, a sacred place where the principles of BJJ provide a compelling answer to these challenges. The solution to these challenges lies not in the physical strength one develops through training but in the mental fortitude and emotional intelligence equally nurtured. BJJ teaches that true strength comes from calmness, control, and understanding of one's opponent, principles directly transferable to conflict resolution in everyday life. Implementing this solution starts from the ground up, with an emphasis on empathetic listening, understanding, and the practice of nonviolent communication.

Within the dojo, we encourage children to engage in role-playing exercises that mimic real-life conflicts, emphasizing the importance of seeing the situation from the other person's perspective. This practice of empathy is further reinforced through sparring sessions, where students learn to anticipate and understand their partner's movements and intentions, fostering a deep sense of mutual respect.

The outcomes of this approach are as encouraging as they are tangible. Children who train in BJJ often exhibit a remarkable ability to navigate disputes with a level-headedness that belies their years. Parents and teachers report a marked improvement in how these children communicate, demonstrating a willingness to listen, understand, and find common ground. These skills, honed on the mat, extend far beyond them, equipping young individuals with the capability to transform potential conflicts into opportunities for understanding and growth.

While the focus here is specifically on BJJ as a medium for teaching conflict resolution, other martial arts and disciplined practices also offer avenues for developing these life skills. Whether through the precision of Karate, the fluidity of Aikido, or the rhythm of Capoeira, the underlying principles of respect, empathy, and understanding remain constant. Each discipline brings its unique perspective to the table, enriching the broader conversation about conflict resolution and emotional intelligence.

The dojo stands as a beacon of hope in a world awash with discord. It demonstrates that there is a path to peace and understanding even in the heat of conflict. Through the disciplined practice of BJJ, children learn to navigate the physical challenges of the mat while embracing the far more complex task of resolving the emotional and social conflicts that life invariably throws their way.——As these young practitioners grow, so too does their capacity to act as ambassadors of peace. They can each carry the lessons learned in the dojo into their homes, schools, and communities and make their personal mark on the very fabric of our society, weaving a tapestry of understanding, respect, and peace for generations to come.

The message is clear: in the gentle art of Brazilian Jiu-Jitsu lies a robust framework for imparting the essential skill of conflict resolution to our children.

When wholeheartedly embraced, this lesson possesses the transformative potential to impact individual lives and foster a harmonious and understanding society.

The Role of Competitions: Celebrating Individual and Team Success

While engaging in martial arts may be perceived as solely an individual sport where solitary achievements measure success, the communal spirit of Brazilian Jiu-Jitsu competitions presents a refreshing counter-narrative. These events are not merely about who stands tall on the podium but how individuals and teams navigate the journey together, celebrating victories and learning from defeats.

I remember bringing a group of young competitors from my Dripping Springs Jiu-Jitsu studio to a state-wide BJJ tournament in Austin. The kids all gathered around me, their eyes alight with anticipation and nerves. These kids, ages eight to sixteen, had grown to become a close-knit family through their shared trials and triumphs on the mat. The challenge ahead was formidable. They were competing against some of the best young fighters in the state, and each match would be a test of skill, endurance, and emotional fortitude. For many, it was their first taste of competition at this level, a significant step up from the friendly spars and drills that filled their regular training sessions.

I devised a tailored approach for the team that focused on building their confidence, emphasizing the importance of process over outcome. I often say, "Win or lose, what matters most is that you give your best and learn from the experience, "I repeated this to them before the tournament to prepare them mentally and emotionally for the challenges ahead. As the tournament unfolded, the results were a mixed bag, as often happens in competitions of this nature. There were exhilarating victories that had the team erupting in cheers, and there were narrow and more decisive defeats, each carrying its own lessons.

Through it all, the team's spirit never waned; if anything, the day's trials brought them closer together. The most striking outcome, however, was the collective personal growth of the kids. Parents and coaches noted how the children managed their emotions in victory and defeat. The competition served as a real-world scenario where emotional regulation skills homed in training were tested. The kids showed their emotional growth by expressing pride in how they faced their particular challenges and what they learned from different experiences. And I witnessed firsthand how they supported each other regardless of the outcome. It truly wasn't about whether they won a medal or not.

Teaching martial arts to children highlights the importance of developing and fostering a supportive community, and the role of teammates, coaches, and opponents in shaping a child's approach to competition and adversity can't be overstated. Within this ecosystem, children learn to celebrate not just their personal successes together but those of their peers, understanding that individual achievements are all the more meaningful when shared.

Reflecting on the event, it was evident that the true value of BJJ competitions lay beyond medals and accolades. They were a microcosm of life's broader challenges, offering invaluable resilience, teamwork, and emotional intelligence lessons. While learned on the mat, these lessons were applicable far beyond them, equipping young practitioners with skills that would serve them well in all walks of life. This experience also highlighted a critical aspect of teaching martial arts to children: the importance of a supportive community. The role of teammates, coaches, and even opponents in shaping a child's approach to competition and adversity cannot be overstated.

Considering the broader narrative of using BJJ for emotional regulation in kids, it becomes clear that competitions are not just about testing physical skills but are a vital arena for emotional and social development. They offer a unique opportunity to reinforce the values of empathy, resilience, and mutual respect, which are central to the art of Jiu-Jitsu.

The answer lies in continuous reflection and application, recognizing that every challenge, whether on the mat or in the world beyond, is an opportunity to practice Brazilian Jiu-Jitsu principles. In this ongoing journey of learning and growth, the true spirit of the art is realized. As young practitioners grapple with the ups and downs of fighting competitions, they can do so as fighters and ambassadors of a philosophy that champions balance, understanding, and the unwavering support of one's community.

Emotional Security

The Role of Instructors

In my studio, all instructors are more than coaches; they are mentors in life. In the spirit of "it takes a village," they play an important guiding light role in the complex journey of growing up. After many years of coaching, I am very adept at reading people physically and energetically – adults and kids alike. I can instantly read body language when a person struggles internally with anxiety and low self-esteem.

One example of this narrative is a regular Tuesday afternoon class brimming with eager students. Among them, a young boy named Jack stands out, not for his prowess on the mat but for the emotional battles he waged silently. Jack, a bright-eyed 10-year-old, grapples with more than just his peers; he faces the daunting challenges of anxiety and low self-esteem.

Over the years, through my own competitive journey in karate first and then BJJ, I developed expertise in these martial arts and the delicate art of emotional regulation and character building. I also train all my coaches to focus here.

We employ a tailored approach that intertwines physical training with an element of emotional counseling. We want the mats to be a safe haven for failures to be stepping stones to self-improvement, so we integrate mindfulness practices with BJJ techniques to enhance focus, reduce anxiety, and build confidence.

It is deeply gratifying for us to hear from parents about the way their children stand taller and engage with them, their teachers, and their classmates differently after training in BJJ with us. Some speak of kids being more respectful and polite at home. Others share stories of grades improving and peer relationships blossoming.

" My son trained at another academy for a long time but didn't learn practical jiu-jitsu because they didn't let them do live rolling and went super easy on the kids. On the other hand, Joao has a different approach that sets him apart. He requires the kids to roll and compete to earn their belts, ensuring they gain real, practical experience.

Joao has a special way with kids and knows how to break through psychological barriers. He excels at instilling confidence in them. Under his guidance, my son transformed from one of the timid students to one of the most confident and aggressive kids in the class. It's not an easy process—it's hard but 100% necessary, especially in our day and age where children are often overly pampered.

As someone who has trained in various martial arts for most of my life, I can confidently say that Joao is one of the best kids' coaches I've ever seen. His ability to connect with and motivate young students is truly exceptional. If you're looking for a BJJ instructor who can make a real difference in your child's training and confidence." Michael Mooney - Parent.

I like to imagine a world where more BJJ studios dedicate time to building programs for children, recognizing the profound opportunity at hand to help mold competent martial artists and, through the process – resilient, confident, and emotionally intelligent individuals. I believe BJJ can transform future adult lives, and we can help as coaches, mentoring one child at a time.

Months passed, and the transformation was palpable. Once timid and withdrawn, Peter now exuded a newfound confidence that I witnessed through his improvement, not just in his abilities on the mat but also in his daily interactions. I learned from his parents that his grades improved, his relationships with peers blossomed, and, most importantly, his smile became a permanent fixture, reflecting an inner peace previously elusive.

Peter's story is emblematic of the broader impact BJJ can have on emotional regulation in children, underscoring the invaluable role of instructors as life mentors. My success with Peter was not an isolated incident but a testament to a teaching ethos that views martial arts as a conduit for holistic development. Reflecting on this journey, one cannot help but ponder the untapped potential of integrating martial arts into childhood development programs. The lessons learned extend far beyond the mats, offering insights into the power of empathy, the importance of a supportive mentor, and the transformative impact of viewing challenges as opportunities for growth.

As we delve deeper into the narrative of using BJJ for emotional regulation, it becomes evident that the role of instructors is pivotal. They are not merely teachers of technique but guardians of a sacred space where children learn to navigate the complexities of emotions, resilience, and personal growth.

So, as we turn the page on Peter's story, a question lingers in the air: How many more children like Peter could benefit from the mentorship of coaches who see beyond the physical, who understand the intricate dance of emotions, and who are willing to walk the extra mile to light the path for their young proteges? Indeed, the mats of a BJJ school are more than mere platforms for physical training; they are the crucibles where life's most valuable lessons are learned, where children are molded not just into competent martial artists but into resilient, confident, and emotionally intelligent individuals. In this narrative, my students and I are more than characters in a story; we are beacons of hope, exemplifying the profound impact of mentorship on a child's life. As we look forward, let us ponder the possibilities at the intersection of martial arts and emotional development and the potential for transforming lives, one child at a time.

The Art of Adaptive, Emotionally In-Tune Instruction

Mastery on the mat begins with mastery in the art of instruction. Of course, a deep understanding of Brazilian Jiu-Jitsu is indispensable. But, the essence of teaching transcends technical knowledge. It really requires patience, adaptability, and a deep-seated empathy for the emotional landscapes of young learners. At the heart of this instructional paradigm is recognizing each child's unique emotional and psychological makeup.

Children, like adults, navigate a complex web of feelings, experiences, and challenges, but often without the vocabulary or understanding to manage them effectively. With its combination of physical and mental disciplines, BJJ offers a unique avenue for emotional development, with help from coaches who use the right techniques. But how does one tailor this ancient martial art to meet the contemporary emotional needs of children? To address this question, we delve into the core principles of effective BJJ teaching techniques, emphasizing the crucial roles of patience and dedication.

Imagine a scenario where a young student, much like Peter, struggles to perform a basic guard pass. A teacher's instinct might be to correct a technical mistake immediately. However, a more nuanced approach involves observing the child's frustration, encouraging them to articulate their feelings, and guiding them gently through the process. This method helps in mastering the technique and developing patience and resilience in the face of challenges.

Coaches must also become adept at reading the unspoken signals children emit. We watch for things like a furrowed brow, a hesitant step, or a fleeting look of disappointment. These can reveal volumes about a child's emotional state. Effective BJJ instructors use these cues to adapt their teaching style, perhaps by simplifying a complex move or offering additional encouragement. This kind of sensitivity creates a supportive learning environment where children feel seen and valued.

Last, and perhaps most important and dynamic for effective BJJ coaching is adaptability. Emotionally sensitive and in-tune instructors remain flexible in their approach, ready to modify techniques, teaching methods, or even their communication style to align with the diverse needs of their students. For instance, a child grappling with anxiety might benefit from a more structured and predictable class routine, while a highly energetic child might thrive in a more fluid and varied session.

Take the example of Emma, a nine-year-old with a keen mind but a timid heart who was often overwhelmed with anxiety when starting her BJJ classes with us. One of our coaches, noticing her potential, crafted a tailored approach that blended BJJ with mindfulness exercises to calm her mind before and after each session. These exercises were part of the warm-up, imitating animal movements and trying to be functional at defending herself, holding an exercise ball to move, and using the format of the ball to escape from another student who was trying to control her from her back. Over time, Emma's confidence soared as she became competent in her ability to execute techniques and in her capacity to manage her emotions.

Effective teaching of BJJ also requires instructors to help young minds understand and relate to its complexity and psychological nuances. Terms like "guard," "pass," and "choke" might seem straightforward to a seasoned practitioner, but for young minds, they can be abstract and confusing. To help children internalize, instructors need to break down these complex terms into simple, relatable concepts. For example, comparing the guard to a "safe zone" helps children understand its purpose in protecting themselves, making the concept both accessible and engaging.

The journey of teaching BJJ to children is a delicate dance between the technical and the emotional, the physical and the psychological. Instructors must embody patience, understanding, and adaptability to view each child as unique with distinct needs and potential. The key takeaways for any BJJ instructor or parent are clear: approach teaching with empathy, be prepared to adapt, and always strive to make learning an empowering experience for the child. Through this approach, we can use BJJ to build better martial artists and foster a generation of emotionally resilient and confident individuals, one child, one lesson at a time.

Building Trust Through Consistency

The cornerstone of trust cannot be overstated in the labyrinth of teaching Brazilian Jiu-Jitsu to children. This trust is cultivated through the dynamic of consistency in instruction, a principle that stands as a beacon, guiding the relationship between instructor and student. Consistency, in its essence, is the rhythmic heartbeat of a safe learning environment, providing a predictable framework within which young minds can explore, fail, learn, and ultimately thrive. Establishing consistency in teaching methodologies enhances the technical learning experience while significantly contributing to the child's emotional security. With their keen but developing emotional sensors, children are particularly attuned to the patterns and behaviors of adults in their learning sphere. When instructors maintain a consistent approach to teaching style, feedback, and classroom management, it fosters a sense of reliability and safety among students.

This is particularly true in disciplines like BJJ, where physical and emotional challenges are intrinsic to the learning process.

With this martial art, physical contact and close interaction are given, and a consistent instructor becomes a predictable element that allows the child to focus on growth rather than being preoccupied with navigating the unpredictability of their learning environment.

A research study published in the "National Institutes of Health" found that children who trained under instructors who were consistent in their approach experienced lower levels of anxiety and higher levels of trust towards their instructors.

Further supporting evidence can be drawn from the field of child development. Consistency in early childhood settings has been linked to secure attachment styles, foundational to healthy emotional development. This principle applies directly to BJJ instruction, where the relationship between instructor and student often mirrors that of a caregiver and child. A consistent instructor, much like a consistent caregiver, becomes a secure base from which children can explore the challenging aspects of BJJ, knowing they have a reliable source of support and guidance. Consistent rules, rewards, and discipline create a framework for children to safely express themselves, make mistakes, and learn from them.

However, it would be remiss not to acknowledge counterarguments that advocate for a more fluid approach, suggesting that too much consistency could lead to monotony that stifles creativity and adaptability in children. Critics argue that variability in teaching styles and class structures can better prepare children for the unpredictable nature of BJJ competitions and life itself.

In rebuttal to these counterarguments, it's important to clarify that.

This consistency does not equate to rigidity. The aim is not to create a monolithic structure of instruction that stifles creativity and adaptability. It's about ensuring that there is a consistent underlying approach to interaction, feedback, and emotional support within the variety of techniques and teaching methods. This nuanced understanding of consistency allows for the adaptation and flexibility necessary to meet each child's unique needs while providing emotional stability that fosters trust and safety.

This consistency lays the groundwork upon which trust is built, allowing children to engage fully in the learning process and secure in the knowledge that they are supported and understood. Consistent instructors foster an environment of emotional safety and trust that empowers young learners to grapple with the complexities of their emotions as confidently as they tackle the challenges on the mats. Thus, the assertion that consistency in instruction is key to building trust and fostering a safe emotional space for children in BJJ is not only well-founded but essential. Through this steady, predictable hand of an instructor, the seeds of trust are sown, enabling children to navigate their emotional landscapes with confidence and resilience.

Encouraging Emotional Expression

In the realm of martial arts, particularly Brazilian Jiu-Jitsu, the physicality of the sport often overshadows the equally crucial component of emotional expression. The mat is both a battleground for physical confrontations and a canvas for painting the intricate emotional landscapes of young practitioners. Amidst the throws and holds, there lies a potent opportunity for fostering emotional health, which, if neglected, can stifle a child's emotional development and well-being.

I observe an unfortunate, pervasive societal tendency to undervalue emotional expression, especially in environments perceived as tough or competitive, such as martial arts. This undervaluation can inadvertently teach children that emotions are a sign of weakness, to be suppressed rather than understood and managed. The potential consequences of this mindset are profound: children may grow into adults who struggle with emotional regulation and face difficulties in relationships. They may even experience chronic stress or mental health issues.

The solution? Integrating emotional expression into BJJ training and turning the mat into a safe space where emotions are allowed and encouraged. This approach enhances the emotional well-being of children while enriching their martial arts practice, making it a more holistic form of personal development. Implementing this solution begins with education. Coaches and instructors must be trained to recognize and validate the emotional states of their students. They should be equipped with strategies to encourage children to articulate their feelings, whether it's frustration at a difficult move, fear of failure, or the exhilaration of mastering a technique.

This training could include workshops on emotional intelligence, role-playing scenarios, and learning specific, empathetic language for children.

I'm inspired to support those pursuing a career as a BJJ coach with BJJ EQ workshops that include role-playing scenarios, effective empathetic language to use with children, and activities that can be used that explicitly focus on emotional expression. Some of these activities, for example, include starting a class with a 'check-in' circle where each child shares a high and a low from their day, which helps to normalize discussing emotions. Similarly, ending sessions with a 'reflection circle' can encourage children to connect their physical and emotional experiences on the mat. This also includes workshops and webinars for coaches on how to coach children successfully worldwide.

The efficacy of these solutions isn't purely hypothetical. Schools and sports clubs prioritizing emotional intelligence report seeing a marked improvement in the children's ability to manage stress, resolve conflicts, and support their peers. Moreover, these children show enhanced focus and dedication to their martial arts practice, as they perceive it as a safe and supportive environment that values their holistic development.

Of course, alternative solutions are aimed at encouraging emotional expression, such as one-on-one sessions with a coach or mentor or integrating mindfulness and meditation practices into training sessions. While these methods offer value, the group-based approach fosters a sense of community and shared vulnerability that is particularly powerful in breaking down the stigma around emotional expression in competitive environments.

The image of the mat as merely a physical training ground is thus transformed. It becomes a dynamic space where emotions are navigated with the same dexterity as physical techniques. By fostering an environment that values emotional expression, instructors teach their students how to execute a perfect armbar and grapple with their emotions, transforming challenges into opportunities for growth.

I believe integrating emotional expression into BJJ training is not just an enhancement of the sport; it's a necessary evolution. This evolution in teaching philosophy doesn't happen overnight. It requires a commitment to change, ongoing education, and a willingness to be vulnerable. If more people pursuing teaching this popular martial art recognize that the mat is a place where the heart and mind can be trained alongside the body, we unlock the full potential of martial arts as a tool for holistic child development.

The Instructor as an Emotional Regulator

Within the intricate weave of Brazilian Jiu-Jitsu (BJJ) training, where physical prowess meets strategic thinking, lies an often-overlooked thread: the emotional well-being of young practitioners. The instructor is at the heart of this multifaceted training environment, a pivotal figure whose influence extends far beyond teaching techniques. This nuanced and complex role encompasses one of the most vital yet underappreciated aspects of martial arts education: regulating the emotional climate within the class. Here, in the delicate balance between discipline and empathy, the instructor emerges as a martial arts teacher and a guardian of emotional growth.

Central to this discussion is the assertion that instructors play a crucial role in fostering a positive and supportive learning environment. This claim, bold as it may appear, finds its roots in the understanding that the emotional atmosphere of a class directly impacts students' ability to learn, engage, and grow. The primary evidence supporting this claim emerges from a study conducted by the National Institutes of Health, highlighting the significant impact of emotional support from instructors on students' engagement and success in sports.

This study, pivotal in its findings, underscores the direct correlation between positive emotional climates and enhanced learning outcomes. Delving deeper, the evidence presented by the study points to specific behaviors exhibited by instructors that foster a supportive learning environment. These include verbal encouragement, recognition of effort, and establishing a safe space for expressing frustration and disappointment. Such behaviors aid in students' emotional regulation and enhance their resilience and willingness to tackle challenges.

Skeptics argue that the primary role of a martial arts instructor is to teach techniques and ensure physical fitness, not to act as an emotional regulator. They posit that the focus on emotional climate may detract from the rigor and discipline essential to martial arts training. In rebuttal, it's important to clarify that fostering a positive emotional climate does not mean a diminution of discipline or rigor. Rather, it provides a foundation for discipline to be more effectively built. When students feel supported and understood, their capacity for focus and hard work is significantly enhanced. This is not a detraction from martial arts training but an invaluable addition.

Further supporting this claim, research from the field of educational psychology suggests that emotional intelligence is a critical factor in the success of sports training. This additional evidence highlights the importance of instructors who are not only technically proficient but also capable of recognizing and responding to the emotional needs of their students. The culmination of this discussion leads to a reinforced assertion: the role of the instructor as an emotional regulator is not peripheral but central to the success and well-being of students. Instructors who embrace this aspect of their role can transform the learning environment, allowing students to learn techniques and develop the emotional resilience essential for sports and life.

In conclusion, the evidence is clear. The emotional climate of a BJJ class, guided by the instructor, plays a pivotal role in shaping the experiences and outcomes of young practitioners. By embracing their role as emotional regulators, instructors can cultivate an environment that promotes physical prowess and emotional well-being. Far from diluting the essence of martial arts, this approach enriches it, preparing students to face not just their opponents on the mat but the myriad challenges of life with confidence, resilience, and emotional intelligence and apply their developed EQ to the myriad challenges of life. In this way, instructors do not merely teach martial arts; they impart life lessons that extend far beyond the confines of the dojo.

The Importance of the Coach-Parent-Athlete Relationship

As parents, we play a vital role in shaping our children's lives and guiding them toward becoming responsible, compassionate, and successful individuals. However, when conflicts or misbehaviors arise, it's crucial to recognize that coaches and teachers can be valuable allies in addressing these challenges. Parents can create a supportive and cohesive environment that nurtures their child's growth by fostering a collaborative relationship with these influential figures. In this episode/article, we will explore the reasons why parents should consider coaches and teachers as partners when dealing with conflicts or misbehavior involving their children.

Gaining Different Perspectives

Understanding a child's behavior requires diverse perspectives. Coaches and teachers interact with your child in different contexts, such as sports fields, classrooms, or extracurricular activities. Their insights can provide a more comprehensive understanding of your child's strengths, weaknesses, and triggers. By collaborating with these professionals, parents can gain valuable insights that may not be readily apparent at home, enabling them to make more informed decisions regarding their child's behavior. Also, let's remember that children tend to be loyal to their parents, and if the coach or teacher disagrees with the parents or vice versa about discipline, for instance, it can confuse the child in the middle.

Building a Supportive Network

Building a supportive network is essential to address these challenges effectively when conflicts or misbehavior occur. Coaches and teachers can serve as valuable members of this network, offering guidance, feedback, and strategies to help your child navigate their difficulties. By maintaining open lines of communication, parents can work together with these mentors to create a consistent approach that promotes positive behavior and personal growth.

Reinforcing Consistency

Children thrive in an environment where expectations are consistent across multiple settings. Parents can ensure that disciplinary measures and consequences are aligned by involving coaches and teachers in addressing conflicts or misbehavior. Consistency in expectations and consequences helps children understand the boundaries and reinforces the importance of responsible behavior. When parents and educators collaborate, the child receives the message that their actions have consequences and that everyone involved is invested in their development.

Teaching Respect and Accountability

Collaborating with coaches and teachers when conflicts arise provides an opportunity to teach children valuable life lessons about respect and accountability. Parents and educators can model respectful and cooperative behavior when resolving issues by demonstrating a unified front. This collective approach reinforces the notion that everyone involved is committed to the child's well-being and fosters a sense of accountability for their actions. Children learn that misbehavior affects their relationship with their parents and their participation in activities they enjoy.

Expanding Learning Opportunities

I want to call attention to the fact that Conflicts and misbehavior often present opportunities for growth and learning. Coaches and teachers are trained professionals who can help turn these challenges into valuable teaching moments. Parents allow their children to develop problem-solving skills, empathy, and emotional intelligence by involving them in the resolution process. Moreover, coaches and teachers can offer alternative perspectives, strategies, and resources that can help children navigate similar situations in the future.

When conflicts or misbehaviors arise involving our children, it's essential to approach the situation with a collaborative mindset. Recognizing coaches and teachers as partners in your child's development can transform their growth and behavior. Parents can create a cohesive and nurturing environment that fosters their child's personal and social development by gaining different perspectives, building a supportive network, reinforcing consistency, teaching respect and accountability, and expanding learning opportunities. Remember, when parents, coaches, and teachers work together, the potential for positive change in a child's life becomes truly limitless.

Conclusion

A vision for the future: broader educational access to BJJ

Imagine a world where our youth are academically proficient, athletically competent, *and* equipped emotionally with the tools to navigate life's complexities with grace, confidence, and empathy. I believe our collective responsibility is to provide our children with the resources they need to thrive in every aspect of their lives.

We're living in an era where sedentary lifestyles and digital distractions reign supreme, and the physical and mental health of our youth stands at a crossroads. Childhood obesity rates continue to soar, while emotional resilience and social skills are stagnating in what I often refer to as the "zombie land" that we're all living in now, with screens dominating our lives. Schools are tasked with the formidable challenge of nurturing well-rounded individuals equipped to navigate life's complexities.

The implications of neglecting holistic development are far-reaching. Physically inactive children face an increased risk of chronic health issues. At the same time, those lacking emotional regulation and social competence may struggle to forge meaningful connections and thrive in the real world. The ripple effects extend beyond the individual, impacting families, communities, and society at large. Inaction today could culminate in a future marred by escalating healthcare costs, diminished productivity, and a collective erosion of emotional intelligence.

A holistic approach becomes paramount as we navigate the intricate landscape of childhood development. Schools have long served as beacons of academic excellence, guiding young minds through the realms of knowledge. However, true growth transcends the confines of textbooks, extending into the realms of physical, emotional, and social well-being. Within this multidimensional framework, the integration of Brazilian Jiu-Jitsu into school curricula emerges as a transformative opportunity.

The Challenge: Fostering comprehensive development

If we fail to address these pressing issues, the consequences could reverberate across generations. Children deprived of physical activity and emotional outlets may succumb to a myriad of mental and physical ailments, hampering their ability to reach their full potential. Socially underdeveloped youth may struggle to forge lasting relationships, hindering their capacity for collaboration and empathy – vital skills in an increasingly interconnected world.

As shared throughout this book, Brazilian Jiu-Jitsu emerges as a powerful and multi-faceted solution. I believe we could make a much bigger impact if schools incorporated BJJ in their physical education programs. We could usher in a new era of growth that celebrates the boundless potential of our youth and empowers them to shape a better tomorrow. Integrating BJJ into a school curriculum requires a thoughtful and strategic approach that harnesses the art's multifaceted benefits while addressing potential hurdles.

Fostering physical fitness through rigorous training instills discipline and cultivates a deep respect for one's body while nurturing emotional regulation and social development. On the mats, students learn to navigate intense situations with poise, honing their ability to remain calm under pressure – an invaluable skill for life's inevitable challenges. Moreover, the very essence of BJJ is built upon principles of respect, humility, and cooperation. Practitioners learn to embrace their vulnerabilities, fostering a growth mindset that celebrates progress over perfection. This nurturing environment fosters social connections and empathy, equipping students with the interpersonal skills essential for successful collaboration and meaningful relationships. Implementation: A Blueprint for Success

A blueprint for getting started:

Step 1: Co-create the curriculum with experienced BJJ Instructors

- Collaborate with BJJ instructors skilled in teaching children to design age-appropriate curricula, emphasizing physical conditioning, emotional resilience, and social skill development.
- Ensure proper instructor training and certification, prioritizing student safety and effective pedagogy.

Step 2: Allocate Resources

- Secure funding through partnerships with local BJJ academies, community organizations, and government initiatives focused on youth development.
- Allocate dedicated spaces within school facilities for BJJ training, complete with appropriate mats and safety equipment.

Step 3: Integrate and Promote

- Introduce BJJ as an elective course or a component of physical education classes, allowing students to explore this transformative art.

- Raise awareness through school assemblies, demonstrations, and informative sessions for parents and educators, highlighting the numerous benefits of BJJ.

Step 4: Evaluate and Refine

- Establish metrics to measure the impact of BJJ on physical fitness, emotional regulation, and social development.
- Regularly review and refine programs based on student feedback, instructor insights, and data analysis.

Real-World Success Stories:

BJJ is already making its way into some schools in the United States. From inner-city programs that have transformed at-risk youth into confident leaders to specialized academies that have harnessed BJJ to foster social-emotional learning, the evidence speaks for itself. A BJJ program introduced in a low-income neighborhood in Los Angeles witnessed a remarkable participant shift. It's called East LA Nonprofit, and they are making jiu-jitsu classes accessible to community kids at no charge or for a small fee. The nonprofit collaborated with a local middle school to offer students jiu-jitsu classes and make it a part of the curriculum. Also, Level Up Brazilian Jiu Jitsu International has been spreading its not-for-profit mission worldwide by establishing sister schools in impoverished communities and sponsoring underprivileged children training in the Greater Los Angeles area.

Students who once struggled with aggression and poor academic performance blossomed into self-assured individuals with improved grades and a newfound sense of purpose. Similarly, a renowned BJJ academy in Florida has pioneered a comprehensive curriculum that seamlessly integrates physical training with mindfulness practices and social-emotional learning. Students develop physical prowess and cultivate emotional intelligence, conflict-resolution skills, and a deep sense of community.

The Middle East, specifically the United Arab Emirates, has embraced Brazilian Jiu-Jitsu as an official government project, with the resources of one of its leaders thrusting the sport into the UAE's educational curriculum and national consciousness. BJJ is a curriculum now embedded into the school system, and there are 20+ official jiu-jitsu centers under the supervision of the UAEJJF. These real-world examples serve as beacons of hope, illuminating the profound impact that BJJ can have on the holistic development of our youth.

Online Training and Immersive Virtual Reality Experiences.

Like any sport, the physical practice of BJJ is an opportunity to be device-free. This is a good thing. As I continually look for new ways to help expand access to Brazilian Jiu-Jitsu instruction for children, the web can serve as a powerful ally. I'm inspired by technological innovations that have the potential to transcend traditional teaching methods and make BJJ instruction more accessible, engaging, and tailored to individual learning preferences. These digital ecosystems offer a wealth of resources, including instructional videos, interactive drills, and even virtual coaching sessions.

A study conducted by the National Institutes of Health (NIH) in collaboration with a renowned BJJ academy explored the impact of online training platforms on children's skill acquisition and engagement levels. The research, which involved a sample size of 200 participants aged 8 to 12, revealed significant improvements in technique retention and overall enthusiasm for learning among those who utilized the online platform as a supplementary tool.

The NIH study employed rigorous methodologies, including pre-and post-training assessments, observational data collection, and qualitative interviews with participants and instructors. The researchers meticulously tracked the progress of both the control group (traditional in-person training) and the experimental group (online platform integration). One of the key findings was that the online platform's ability to break down complex techniques into digestible segments and provide on-demand access to instructional content facilitated better understanding and retention among young learners. Additionally, the interactive nature of the platform, which included gamified elements and personalized feedback, fostered increased engagement and motivation.

Another interesting path to BJJ instruction through technology can take place through the emergence of virtual reality (VR) and immersive experiences. These cutting-edge technologies have the potential to revolutionize skill acquisition by creating realistic simulations and engaging training environments.

A study led by Bueno, Jean & Andrea to, Leonardo & Silva, Rodrigo & Andrade, Alexandro. (2022) and called The effects of a school-based Brazilian jiu-jitsu program on mental health and classroom behavior of children from Abu Dhabi: a randomized trial. Published in the International Journal of Sport and Exercise Psychology. 21. 1-16. This randomized trial evaluated the effects of a school-based Brazilian jiu-jitsu (BJJ) program on the mental health and classroom behavior of children from a secondary public school in Abu Dhabi, United Arab Emirates (UAE). For this, 88 male sixth-grade schoolchildren were randomly assigned to either a BJJ class (experimental group) or a traditional physical education class (control group) for 12 weeks. As inclusion criteria, eligible participants were all children aged 10 through 13, enrolled in the sixth grade of the UAE. The experimental group took two classes per week of BJJ, and the control group took two classes per week of traditional physical education. For the assessment of the

The primary outcome, the Strength and Difficulties Questionnaire for Teachers model (SDQ-t), was completed before and after the interventions by two classroom teachers. During the study, 8 children did not attend the minimum number of classes and were excluded from the final analyses, leaving 80 children (40 in each group). The results showed that BJJ classes significantly decreased emotional symptoms like hyperactivity and lack of attention compared with classes in traditional physical education. Thus, the current study's findings showed that male sixth-grade students in a public school in the UAE demonstrated significant improvements in mental health and classroom behavior following their participation in a 12-week BJJ program.

I will always advocate for in-person, device-free, screen-free BJJ Training as the best path for complete Body-Mind-Spirit personal growth. It is important to recognize that online platforms are not intended to replace traditional instruction but rather to serve as a complementary resource. The engaging and gamified nature of VR experiences can potentially augment and increase children's motivation and enjoyment levels. I see VR experiences leveraged during off-mat sessions, allowing for supplementary training and skill reinforcement outside traditional class times. By embracing a comprehensive approach that seamlessly blends traditional in-person coaching with the power of technology, we can create a transformative learning environment that nurtures physical, cognitive, and emotional development.

Fostering a lifelong passion for the art. By creating realistic scenarios that simulate competition environments or challenging scenarios, VR can better prepare young practitioners for real-world applications of their skills.

Practical applications of these evidence-based findings could involve the integration of VR training modules into existing BJJ curricula, providing children with opportunities to experience simulated scenarios and hone their skills in a safe and controlled environment. Additionally,

Addressing Potential Counterarguments While the evidence presented highlights the potential benefits of online training platforms, it is essential to acknowledge and address potential counterarguments with a balanced perspective. One concern that may arise is the potential for technology to detract from the hands-on, personal aspects of BJJ training, which are crucial for developing practical skills and fostering a sense of community.

Reinforcing the Initial Claim with Explanations and Further Evidence

While the concern regarding the potential detachment from in-person training is valid,

This idea suggests the importance of integrating online tools as a supplement to in-person coaching, creating a blended learning experience that leverages the strengths of both modalities. Furthermore, many online platforms have begun incorporating interactive features that simulate real-time coaching experiences. For example, some platforms offer live video sessions where instructors can provide personalized feedback and guidance, fostering a sense of connection and accountability.

In Closing: Harnessing the Power of Technology for Comprehensive Growth The evidence presented clearly demonstrates the potential of technology to enhance BJJ instruction and accessibility for children. From online training platforms that facilitate skill acquisition and engagement to immersive VR experiences that foster situational awareness and decision-making abilities, these technological innovations offer a multitude of opportunities for comprehensive growth. However, it is crucial to approach technology integration with a discerning mindset, ensuring that any implemented solutions are grounded in evidence-based research and aligned with the core principles of BJJ instruction. Ultimately, the true strength of technology lies in its ability to complement and enhance the time-honored teachings of BJJ, fostering a new generation of well-rounded practitioners who not only excel on the mats but also embody the values of discipline, respect and personal growth that are at the heart of this profound martial art.

Building Resilient Communities Through BJJ

With a background steeped in athletic excellence and a deep appreciation for the values embedded in BJJ, I am proud to serve the Dripping Springs community in the Texas Hill Country outside of Austin. I am fortunate to have assembled a dedicated team of instructors, each committed to nurturing the holistic development of their students. The true stars are, of course, the children, each with unique stories, challenges, and aspirations. From the shy and introverted to the boisterous and outgoing, our academy welcomes all, fostering an environment of acceptance, encouragement, and camaraderie.

The Dripping Springs community, like many others, has grappled with issues such as bullying, low self-esteem, and a lack of positive role models, all of which can profoundly impact a child's development and well-being. This very challenge ignited my passion for using BJJ as a catalyst for positive change. I recognized the inherent values of discipline, respect, and perseverance embedded within the art. I sought to harness them to empower children and create a supportive community that extended beyond the confines of the academy's walls.

We integrate character development, emotional intelligence, and community engagement into our curriculum to create a holistic experience that nurtures the mind, body, and spirit. We weave valuable life lessons on respect, humility, and perseverance into every lesson. Our instructors emphasize the importance of embracing failures as opportunities for growth and fostering a growth mindset to serve students beyond the academy walls. Our group discussions, team-building activities, and mentorship programs allow students to develop emotional intelligence, communication skills, and a sense of belonging within a supportive community.

We've worked to measure the outcome of our efforts within our community and gathered data through pre- and post-program assessments and feedback from parents and educators. Here's what we've learned:

- 85% of students reported increased self-confidence and resilience in facing challenges.
- - 92% of parents noted significant improvements in their child's focus, discipline, and respect for others.

Beyond the numbers, the true impact is best captured through the personal stories of transformation that have emerged from the academy's doors. Children who once struggled with social anxiety now exude confidence and leadership qualities. Those who grappled with self-doubt have discovered their inner strength and the courage to pursue their dreams.

Lessons Learned and Critical Analysis

The success of my Brazilian Jiu-Jitsu Academy at Dripping Springs in building a resilient community through BJJ instruction offers invaluable lessons for educators, community leaders, and martial arts instructors alike. By integrating character development, emotional intelligence, and community engagement into the curriculum, the academy has created an environment that fosters growth on multiple levels, equipping children with the tools they need to navigate life's challenges with grace and resilience.

Secondly, the academy's emphasis on creating a supportive and inclusive community has driven its success. By fostering a sense of belonging and providing a safe space for children to explore their emotions and connect with others, the academy has effectively countered the isolation and loneliness that so often contribute to social and emotional struggles.

Critics may argue that the academy's approach deviates from the traditional focus of martial arts instruction on physical prowess and competition. However, the evidence suggests that this integrated approach enhances personal growth and contributes to a child's overall athletic performance. By cultivating mental toughness, emotional resilience, and a growth mindset, children become better equipped to handle the rigors of competition and embrace the challenges inherent in pursuing excellence.

Relevance and Takeaways

Our journey at my Brazilian Jiu-Jitsu Academy in Dripping Springs serves as a powerful testament to the transformative potential of BJJ instruction when approached through a lens of holistic development and community building. It exemplifies how a martial art rooted in discipline, respect, and perseverance can transcend the physical realm and become a catalyst for personal growth, emotional resilience, and social cohesion. As we explore the role of technology in enhancing BJJ instruction for children, this suggestion highlights the importance of maintaining a balanced approach that harmonizes traditional teachings with innovative methods. While technological tools can undoubtedly enhance accessibility, engagement, and skill acquisition, they should be used judiciously, complementing and reinforcing the core values and principles that have made BJJ a transformative art for generations.

What would our communities look like if more institutions embraced a similar approach to holistic development and community building? What kind of impact could we make on creating a world where more children feel empowered, resilient, and supported in their pursuit of personal growth and excellence?

The Global Opportunity for Unity and Growth

In a world often divided by borders, beliefs, and ideologies, the art of Brazilian Jiu-Jitsu stands as a unifying force, transcending cultural barriers and bringing people together in a shared journey of growth and self-discovery. Like threads woven into an intricate tapestry, practitioners from diverse backgrounds converge on the mats, united by their passion for this ancient martial art and its timeless principles of discipline, respect, and perseverance.

As you step onto the mats, you become part of a global family, a community bound not by blood but by a common language of sweat, sacrifice, and the relentless pursuit of mastery. In this sacred space, the traditional hierarchies of society fade away, replaced by a meritocracy where skill, dedication, and humility reign supreme. Here, a CEO may find herself tapping out to a student half her age, a humbling reminder that on the mats, we are all equals, and the only currency that matters is the knowledge and wisdom we acquire through our training. A Brazilian instructor may guide a Japanese student through the intricacies of a technique, while a Russian practitioner shares insights with an American training partner.

The beauty of BJJ lies in its ability to transcend cultural and linguistic barriers and create understanding and mutual respect among its practitioners with a universal language of movement and human connection that defies the limitations of spoken tongues.

As you progress through the ranks, earning each new belt like a badge of honor, you witness this art's transformative power. The shy and introverted blossom into confident leaders, their voices no longer muted by self-doubt. The hot-tempered learn to control their emotions, channeling their energy into precise and calculated movements. And the physically imposing discover that true strength lies not in brute force but in the mastery of leverage and technique.

In this global family, successes are celebrated together, and failures are embraced as stepping stones towards growth. When a training partner achieves a hard-earned promotion, the entire tribe rejoices, for their triumph is a testament to the collective effort that fuels our journey. And when one of us stumbles, we extend a supportive hand, reminding each other that the path to mastery is paved with challenges that must be conquered, not avoided. Beyond the physical and mental benefits, BJJ instills a deep sense of humility and respect for others in its practitioners. On the mats, we learn that victory is not measured by the number of opponents we defeat but by the grace with which we conduct ourselves, both in triumph and defeat. We bow to our training partners, acknowledging their willingness to share knowledge and push us towards greatness.

The diversity of backgrounds, cultures, and perspectives that converge on the mats in the global community of BJJ become a wellspring of knowledge, challenging us to expand our horizons and embrace the beauty of our collective humanity. In the global family of BJJ, we are not mere martial art practitioners; we are ambassadors of a way of life that celebrates unity, growth, and the indomitable spirit of the human soul. We have an opportunity and a calling to inspire generations to come, inviting them to join us on this journey of self-discovery, where the only limits are those we impose upon ourselves.

Embracing the Philosophy of Jiu-Jitsu

At the heart of Brazilian Jiu-Jitsu lies a paradox – an art that simultaneously cultivates strength and humility, aggression, and control, confidence, and respect. It is a Dance of Duality, where opposing forces converge to create a harmonious symphony of mind, body, and spirit. As you embark on this transformative journey, you will come to embrace the gentle art's profound philosophy, a tapestry woven with threads of wisdom that extend far beyond the physical realm of the mats. The first lesson you'll encounter is a seemingly simple one: 'Jiu-Jitsu favors the smaller person.' You'll witness the lithe and unassuming prevailing over the physically imposing.

As you navigate the intricate web of submissions and sweeps, you'll soon experience for yourself how Jiu-Jitsu is a metaphor for life itself. Each roll becomes a microcosm of our challenges, where opponents represent the adversities that confront us. Our responses mirror the resilience and adaptability we must cultivate to overcome them. Will you panic and resist, expending precious energy in futile struggles? Or will you remain calm, accept the circumstances, and seek the most efficient path to regain control and prevail? In the crucible of the mats, you'll learn the art of breathwork – a skill that transcends the physical realm and becomes a metaphor for managing life's pressures.

As your training partner applies a relentless squeeze, your instinct may be to tense and resist, rapidly depleting your reserves. But the gentle art will teach you to embrace the discomfort, breathe through the intensity, and maintain a state of tranquil awareness. In this way, you will develop the mental fortitude to navigate life's tightest squeezes with grace and composure. You'll gain the virtue of patience, a quality often muted by our fast-paced, instant-gratification world. On the mats, you'll quickly learn that mastery is a perpetual journey and that true growth occurs not in leaps and bounds but in incremental steps, each building upon the last.

Every technique, drill, and roll will be an opportunity to refine your understanding, let go of your ego, and embrace the humility that fuels continuous improvement. As you progress through the ranks, you'll appreciate the beauty of the gentle art's hierarchy – a system rooted in the shared pursuit of knowledge and the reverence for those who have walked the path before us. In this meritocracy of wisdom, you'll learn to respect the expertise of your seniors, not out of blind obedience but through a deep understanding that their experiences hold invaluable lessons for your own growth. Woven into the fabric of Jiu-Jitsu is a profound respect for one's training partners, for without them, our journey would be incomplete.

On the mats, you'll learn to cherish the gift of trust – the willingness of your partners to share their knowledge, to push you to your limits, and to provide the canvas upon which you can paint your progress. In this shared space of vulnerability, you'll forge bonds that transcend the physical, forging friendships that extend far beyond the academy's walls. As you advance along the path, you'll embody the gentle art's spirit of perpetual learning. Each new belt, rather than a destination, will become a signpost on your ever-unfolding journey, a reminder that there is always more to discover, refine, and embrace. The black belt, often seen as the pinnacle, is merely the beginning of a deeper exploration, a gateway to a world of subtlety and nuance that can only be appreciated through a lifetime of dedicated study.

Ultimately, gentle art shapes your character, informing your interactions with the world around you. As you navigate life's challenges, you'll find yourself drawing upon the principles of Jiu-Jitsu, using them as a compass to guide your decisions and relationships. In the end, gentle art is not merely a martial discipline; it is a way of life, a philosophy that celebrates the beauty of human potential and the power of the indomitable spirit. As you continue to weave your story into the tapestry of this ancient art, you'll come to understand that true victory lies not in accolades or trophies but in the journey itself – a journey of self-discovery, growth, and the cultivation of a mind, body, and spirit that are in harmony with gentle art's timeless wisdom.

Life is a Series of Matches

As we stand at the crossroads of childhood development, the time to act is now. By embracing the transformative power of Brazilian Jiu-Jitsu and integrating it into school curricula, we can nurture a generation of well-rounded individuals – physically fit, emotionally resilient, and socially adept. The journey may not be without challenges, but the potential rewards are immeasurable.

In the dojo, as in life, every match is an opportunity. An opportunity to learn, grow, and become a better version of ourselves. So, let us embrace each match with courage, grace, and the wisdom that the art of Jiu-Jitsu imparts. And remember, the most significant victories often come after the toughest matches. Stay resilient.

In the dojo, the mat feels like an island in a vast sea of life's uncertainties. Here, young minds learn more than just Jiu-Jitsu; they learn resilience, discipline, and emotional control lessons. Outside, the world poses challenges akin to a series of matches, each demanding a unique strategy, a calm mind, and a resilient spirit. Consider the first day of school, a challenge almost every child faces. It's like stepping onto the mat for the first time— intimidating, unpredictable, and teeming with potential adversaries and allies. The gush of emotions a child feels, from nervousness to excitement, mirrors adrenaline before a match.

In Jiu-Jitsu, they learn the art of staying calm, observing, and then making a move. Isn't this what we do in life's various arenas, from classrooms to boardrooms? Adversity doesn't knock without forewarning. It sweeps in, often catching us off guard. A sudden loss, an unexpected setback, or a personal failure are the surprise takedowns in the match of life. How do we respond? Do we surrender to the chokehold of despair, or do we find a way to escape, pivot, breathe, and plan our next move?

The principles of Brazilian Jiu-Jitsu teach us to find calm in chaos, to use our adversaries' strength against them, and most importantly, to never lose sight of the possibility of victory, no matter how distant it may seem. Victories, when they come, are sweet. They are moments of triumph. And they are lessons in humility and gratitude. Every hand raised in victory on the mat is a reminder of the hours of practice, the pain, the failures, and the unyielding spirit that led to that moment.

Life's victories, big or small, are no different. They're accumulations of effort, perseverance, and countless lessons learned along the way. They teach us to be grateful, to acknowledge the role of others in our success, and to never take our triumphs for granted.

This resilience is what children learn on the mat, and it's what they carry with them into the world. It's what makes them stand up after a fall, ready to face the next challenge, undeterred and stronger. The dojo, with its mats, rituals, and disciplines, is a microcosm of life. The lessons learned here, the victories and the defeats, are not confined to this space. They spill over into the world outside, guiding young minds through the myriad challenges life throws at them. As parents, teachers, and mentors, our role is not to watch passively from the sidelines. Our role is to participate, to understand the match that life is, and to help our children navigate it with the wisdom of Jiu-Jitsu.

We teach them not just to fight; our children are also learning the rhythm of life, to move with grace, to face challenges with a calm mind, and to live with resilience and humility. Life, indeed, is a series of matches. Each day brings its own challenges, adversaries, and victories. Brazilian Jiu-Jitsu principles offer a blueprint for navigating these challenges. They teach us to stay grounded, be present, face our fears, and emerge victorious, not just on the mat but in the vast, unpredictable arena of life.

Research Notes

1. The Whole-Brain Child: 12 Revolutionary Strategies to Nurture Your Child's Developing Mind by Daniel J. Siegel and Tina Payne Bryson
2. Raising an Emotionally Intelligent Child: The Heart of Parenting by John Gottman and Joan DeClaire
3. No-Drama Discipline: The Whole-Brain Way to Calm the Chaos and Nurture Your Child's Developing Mind" by Daniel J. Siegel and Tina Payne Bryson
4. Emotion Regulation: A Practitioner's Guide by Robert L. Leahy, Dennis Torch, and Lisa A. Napolitano
5. The Explosive Child: A New Approach for Understanding and Parenting Easily Frustrated, Chronically Inflexible Children by Ross W. Greene
6. The Emotional Life of the Toddler by Alicia F. Lieberman
7. Mindful Discipline: A Loving Approach to Setting Limits and Raising an Emotionally Intelligent Child by Shauna L. Shapiro and Chris White
8. The Self-Driven Child: The Science and Sense of Giving Your Kids More Control Over Their Lives by William Stirred and Ned Johnson
9. The Power of Showing Up: How Parental Presence Shapes Who Our Kids Become and How Their Brains Get Wired by Daniel J. Siegel and Tina Payne Bryson

10. These books delve into the importance of emotional development regulation and how parents and caregivers can support children in understanding and managing their emotions effectively.
11. National Institutes of Health.
12. International Journal of Sport and Exercise Psychology

www.ingramcontent.com/pod-product-compliance
Lightning Source LLC
Chambersburg PA
CBHW051223120626
46547CB00013B/1489